AF605053

ANYA goes to NIGERIA

written by NIKKO FUNGCHUNG
illustrations by FUUJI TAKASHI

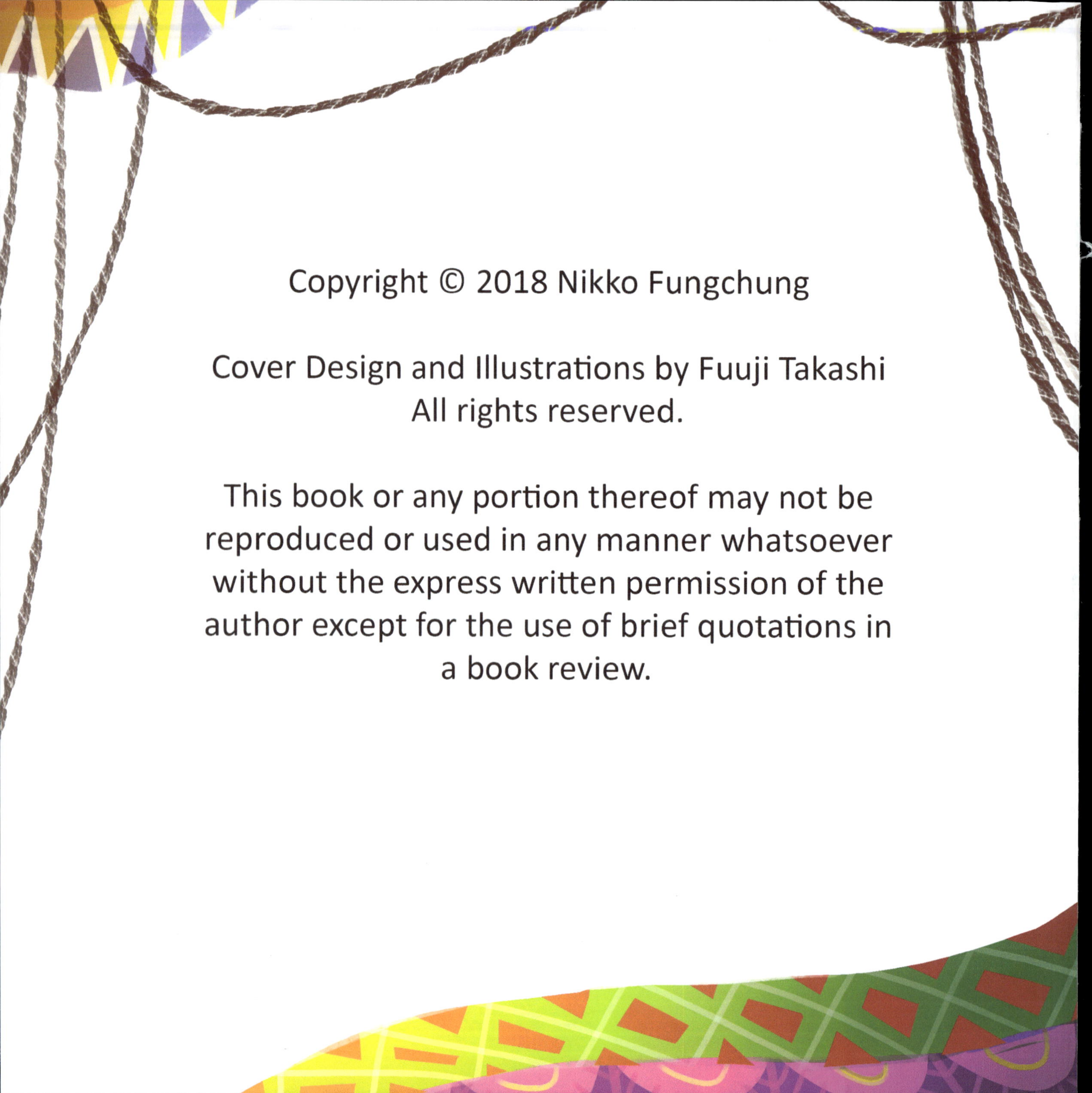

Cover Design and Illustrations by Fuuji Takashi

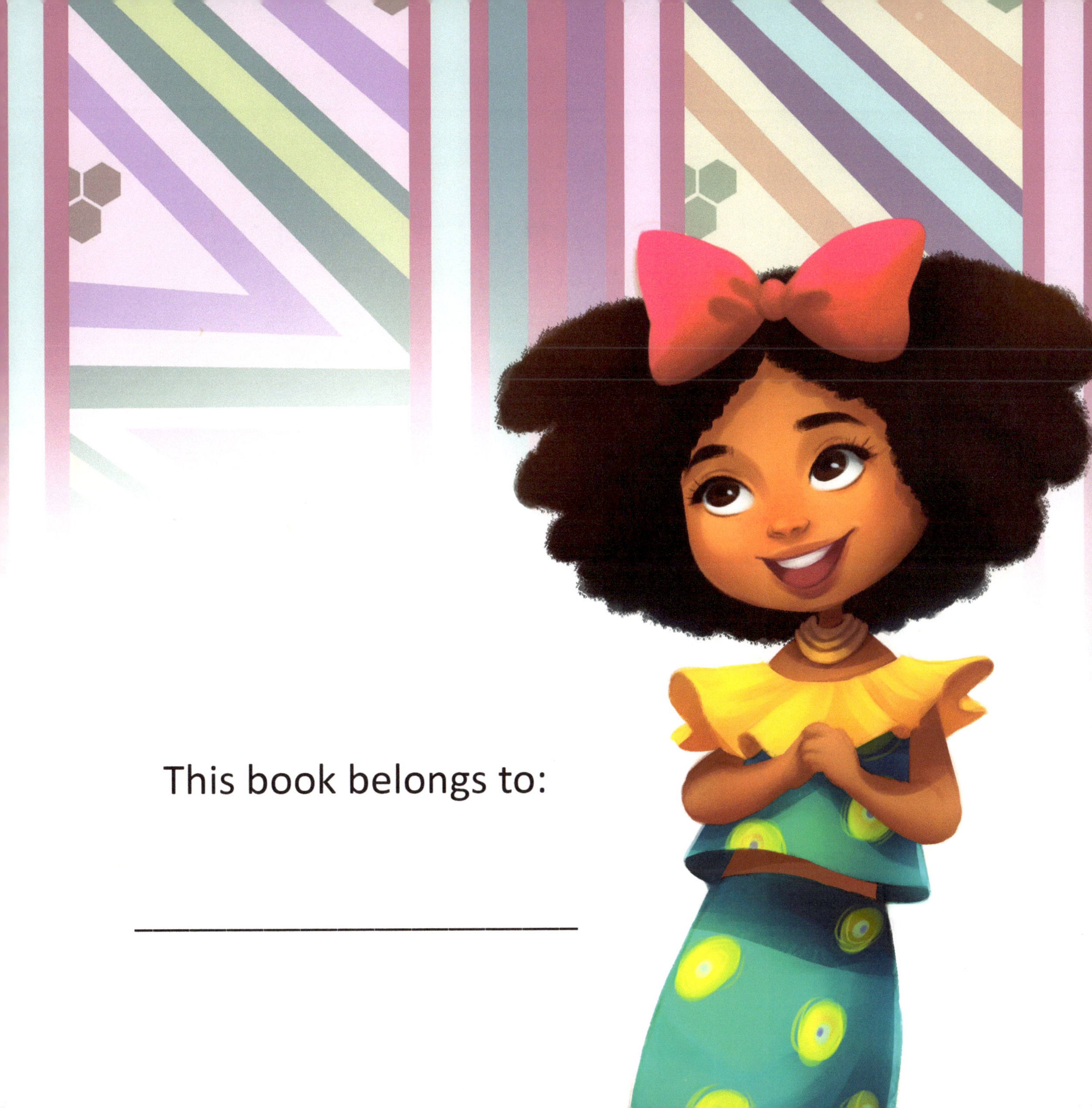

This book belongs to:

____

"A child who is carried on the back will not know how far the journey is."

Nigerian Proverb

My name is Anya and I am a world traveler! I love to visit new places and learn about different cultures.

This is my magic globe!
It takes me on exciting adventures
all around the world!

My favorite part about visiting new places is getting to know the people who live there.

I love learning what they eat.
I love learning how they play.
I love learning what they wear.
I love learning how they do their hair.

When I'm ready to take a trip, I close my eyes tight and spin my globe like this...

Wow! We've landed in the country of Nigeria! Nigeria is located on the Western Coast of the African continent.

The Nigerian flag is green and white.
The country's capital is Abuja.

Nigeria is divided into 36 states with over 250 ethnic groups. Each group has their own language and heritage.

The country's official language is English. Hausa, Igbo, and Yoruba are also very common languages throughout the nation.

Nigeria has a tropical climate with only two seasons.

The Dry Season brings hot temperatures and dry air.
The Wet Season brings heavy rains and cooler days.

Lagos is the most populated city in Nigeria. It is one of the fastest growing cities in Africa for business and technology.

The city of Lagos is made up of the mainland and an island connected by a long bridge. Like many large cities around the world, Lagos is known for it's culture and excitement!

I have a friend named Anwuli who lives in the suburb of Ikeja, Lagos.

Anwuli lives with her brother Golibe, her baby sister Iben, her mom and dad.

Anwuli's mom makes us
some akara for snack.
It is delicious!

After we eat, her dad and brother teach me to play a game called Ayoayo.

The rules are simple, but you have to play wise to win.

The goal is to capture the most beads in your bin.

Today, we are going to the Felabration music festival.

It is a yearly celebration
of Afrobeat music and its
creator, Fela Kuti.

I really enjoy the music and dancing with my friends. The singer on stage is wearing a beautiful gele and a matching dress.

I imagine myself in a beautiful pink and yellow gele and dress.

There are lots of tasty foods to try at Felabration. I'm having suya, boli and roasted corn.

Everything tastes great!

It’s getting late, but before I go, we will drive down to Lekki Market to get a souvenir to take home.

Nigeria is such a diverse and inviting country.

I enjoyed the music, the food, the games and the fashion too.

What I liked most of all was sharing it with you.

Here is something special, so you will always remember our adventure.

See you next time...
wherever the magic globe takes us!

The adventure continues at

www.AWABookSeries.com